THE VIRGIN MARY

Also in this series by the same author:

THE CELEBRATION OF FAITH

Volume 1: *I Believe...*
Volume 2: *The Church Year*

THE VIRGIN MARY

The Celebration of Faith

Sermons, Volume 3

by
ALEXANDER SCHMEMANN

Foreword by
PAUL MEYENDORFF

*with selections translated
from the Russian by*
JOHN A. JILLIONS

ST VLADIMIR'S SEMINARY PRESS
Crestwood, NY 10707–1699
1995

> *The publication of this book has been underwritten through the generosity of Mr. and Mrs. Alexander Hixon.*

Library of Congress Cataloging-in-Publication Data

THE VIRGIN MARY
Celebration of Faith

English language translation
Copyright © 1995

by

ST VLADIMIR'S SEMINARY PRESS

ISBN 0–88141–141-8
ISBN 0-88141-145-0 (Set)

PRINTED IN THE UNITED STATES OF AMERICA

Contents

Foreword

This volume comprises the third volume of sermons by Father Alexander Schmemann, on a topic which was particularly close to his heart. The Virgin Mary, usually referred to as "Theotokos" among the Orthodox, figures prominently in Byzantine liturgical worship. There is no single service which does not contain one or more references to her. Yet Eastern Orthodox theological manuals have little to say about Mary beyond repeating the primarily *Christological* titles affirmed by the Third Ecumenical Council (Ephesus, 431)—"Theotokos," "Birthgiver of God." It is to the Eastern liturgical tradition, then, that one must turn for a more developed Mariology. Eastern hymnographers, drawing both on Scripture, on early Christian apocrypha, as well as on a rich thological tradition, went far beyond the laconic definition of Ephesus. In these brief pages, Father Schmemann draws on all these to explain Mariology to a modern audience.

The first section, entitled "The Mother of God," consists of a series of sermons, originally delivered in Russian over Radio Liberty and translated here for the first time. The message is direct and simple, addressed to a largely unchurched audience in the former Soviet Union.

The second part of this volume, comprising chapters two through five, is quite different. Here, Father Schmemann addresses a western audience in a series of academic lectures originally published in *Marian Studies* and *The University of Dayton Review*, some three decades ago. With this edition, they are now made available to a more general audience.

Paul Meyendorff

1

The Mother of God

Introduction

I am certain that both unbelievers and Christian believers are fully aware of the immense and utterly unique role that veneration of Mary, the Mother of Jesus, plays in Christian faith and Church life. Since earliest times, Church tradition has called her the Mother of God, the Birth-Giver of God, the Most Pure, the All-Holy... In one of the most widespread and widely used prayers she is praised as "more honorable than the Cherubim and incomparably more glorious than the Seraphim." There is no service and almost no prayer in which her name is not mentioned. And her presence in art alone demands our attention since no image so permeates Christian art of East and West as the image of Mother and Child. As soon as we enter an Orthodox Church we see this icon in its place of honor next to the central doors of the icon screen (the "Royal Doors"), and just in front of it a candlestand with a sea of burning candles. Looking up toward the apse, the wall above and behind the altar, the image of Mary is often seen at the center, as if she were the heart of the world, with an inscription: "All of Creation rejoices in You, O Full of Grace." In Russia alone there used to be more than three hundred "wonder-working" icons of the Mother of God that were accorded extraordinary veneration. A continuous stream of prayers, praise, petitions, joy, and exceptional devotion flowed toward her.

Today however, many people, even among those

who, as we say today, are "interested" in religion and have come from atheism to faith, question the meaning of venerating the Mother of Jesus Christ. To them, her veneration is no longer self-evident; on the contrary, it is even regarded as problematic. To worship God and Christ is understandable. But hasn't Mary been given too much attention and hasn't her icon overshadowed the icon of her Son in popular piety? Hasn't this praise and devotion been exaggerated beyond all reasonable proportion? Here I'm not speaking of unbelievers or atheists or active opponents of religion. To them, this entire cult, this "Mother cult" or "Virgin cult," as they call it, is from beginning to end nothing but superstition and folk custom, the remnants of ancient pagan worship of Mother Earth and Nature and its forces of regeneration.

But Christians themselves are asking these questions, and therefore it is all the more essential that we attempt to explain the genuine meaning, content and orientation of the Church's ancient and continuing glorification of the One who said of herself, "For behold, henceforth all generations will call me blessed" (Lk 1:48). I say "attempt," because it is no easy task to give such an explanation. As one of the hymns for the Annunciation says, "Let no impure hand touch the living temple of God." The more elevated, the more pure, the more holy, the more beautiful the subject one wants to speak about, the more difficult it is. And to me it seems impossible for words to fully express precisely what, in this singular image of Mother and Child, church consciousness has in all ages seen, understood, and come to love and glorify with such joy and tenderness.

Why Do We Venerate the Mother of God?

The New Testament says very little about Mary, the Mother of Jesus Christ. Of the four evangelists, only two, Matthew and Luke, tell of Jesus Christ's birth in Bethlehem, mention His mother and describe the circumstances. Mark does not mention Mary at all. In John's gospel she appears only twice: at the very beginning, where in the story of the marriage at Cana in Galilee she intercedes with her Son on behalf of the banquet's stewards when the wine runs out (Jn 2:1-11), and at the very end of the Gospel where she appears once again, standing by the Cross of her crucified Son. The Acts of the Apostles (which in its first half describes life in the earliest Christian community at Jerusalem) mentions Mary only once, in the first chapter, saying that the disciples of Christ were gathered in prayer "together with the women and Mary, the Mother of Jesus..." (Acts 1:14). In none of the remaining New Testament books, in none of the letters of St Paul or of the other apostles is anything at all said about her.

The relative silence of the New Testament is put forward as the main argument by those who view with skepticism the vast and pivotal role that Church life has given to the veneration of the Mother of God. They see this as something "imported" and foreign to Christianity's original spirit and teaching. This was the argument of sixteenth-century Protestants who concluded that the veneration and devotion shown to the Mother of God was pure idol worship without any basis in Holy Scriptures. "Your Church," we are still told, "celebrates the Birth of the Mother of God, her Entrance Into the Temple, her Dormition. But none of these events is even mentioned in the Holy Scriptures, the Bible, the New Testament, and so all these feasts are human inventions that have tainted the original purity and simplicity of Christian teaching."

This is a very serious challenge, and so we start here in our attempt to explain the content and meaning of Christian and Church veneration of Mary. But first I must say a few words concerning the general approach to religious phenomena as a whole, for there have always been two approaches. One could be called the external approach, the other is the approach from within.

The simplest definition of the external approach is that it depends entirely on proof. "Prove that God exists, prove that Christ is God, prove that bread becomes the Body of Christ, prove that there is another world... Prove it, and then I will believe you. But unless you prove it, I will not believe." It is enough merely to reflect on all these "proves" to be convinced that not only is this approach incapable of leading us to the essence of religion, but also, with the exception of the relatively narrow field of natural sciences, it is entirely unsuited to life in general. You can prove that water boils at 100 degrees C., but you can't prove that Pushkin is a genius. And it is just as impossible to prove anything that concerns the inner world and life of man, his joys and sorrows, his wonder and faith. Note that Christ himself made no attempt to prove anything, He only called people to see, to hear, to accept something they could neither see, nor hear, nor accept, and which even now the great majority of people do not see, hear or accept. In other terms, the more profound the truth, the good, the beauty, the less can it be proven, and therefore an approach limited to proofs becomes less and less applicable. This brings us to the method I called the approach from within.

This is the method we all use in our day to day lives without even being aware of it. So, for example, when we love a person, we see something in him or her that someone who doesn't love them cannot see. Something of their inner being is revealed to us, something hidden from external sight but uncovered by love, intimacy, personal knowledge. In the same way, in our attempt to understand the Church's devotion to Mary, rather than count how many times the Mother of Jesus is mentioned in this or that text, we can ask the question in a completely different way, using the method "from within." Let me put it this way: if our faith in Christ knew nothing of His Mother except that she existed and that her name was Mary, then even this most elementary knowledge would be enough to genuinely know her, to behold in her image, to find within Christian faith, and to find likewise within our own hearts all that the Church has seen, heard, and come to know of her in two thousand years. We are told that the Bible says nothing about Mary's birth or death. But if she existed, then she must have been born, she must have died. Can our love for Christ and our faith in Him be so lukewarm as to have no feeling for what took place when she gave birth, that we have no feeling for the One whose purpose in life was to be His Mother? If we believe in the absolute, divine uniqueness of Christ and His work, then how can we not focus our inner, spiritual sight on the woman who gave Him his human life? In other words, all our veneration of the Mother of God, all our love for her, all our knowledge of her is a gift that comes solely through personal experience, as the fruit of love. And if we genuinely desire to understand the Church's veneration of Mary, then we have only one choice: come, taste and decide for ourselves if all this is invention and myth, or if indeed truth, life, and beauty disclose to us their own vitality, depth and grace.

The Ever Virgin

The Church honors Mary's perpetual virginity and daily addresses her in prayer as Virgin: "Mother of God, Virgin, Mary, full of grace, rejoice, the Lord is with you..." Many people obviously regard this faith in the virgin birth as a stumbling block, " a stone that will make men stumble, a rock that that will make them fall" (Rom 9:33; cf. Is 8:14). It is a source of doubt and confusion for them and justifies their view of Christianity as a collection of superstitions. Believers ususally respond to these doubts by calling the virgin birth a miracle that we believe in, that must be taken on faith and is beyond understanding...

While this may be self-evident to believers, it is absolutely necessary to elaborate the answer more precisely. On the one hand, it makes sense that if, as Christians believe, there is a God who is Creator of the world and life and all its natural laws, then this God must be all-powerful and capable of reversing these laws. In other terms, He must be capable of performing what are popularly known as miracles. A miracle is something that takes place beyond the limits of those familiar laws of nature, something we experience as "supernatural" rather than "natural." If God is God, then clearly He is infinitely beyond all "rules of nature," He is all-powerful, omnipotent and absolutely free to act as He desires.

While this is all true—and faith which denies the miraculous and makes God subject to the limited laws of nature is no longer faith—it does not mean that we, as believing Christians, are forbidden to ask ourselves and our faith about the meaning of miracles. For there is a distinctly Christian understanding of the miraculous, coming from the Gospels and Christ Himself, which requires particular spiritual attention if it is to be understood. To begin with, the image we have of Christ in the Gospels does preclude the view of miracles as "proofs," as factual tools to force someone into belief. Indeed, if anything in Christ's unique image is predominant, then it is His extreme humility and not at all any desire to "prove" his Divinity by using miracles. The Apostle Paul writes some extraordinary words about this humility of Christ: "He was in the form of God...but emptied Himself, taking the form of a servant... He humbled Himself and became obedient unto death, even death on a cross..." (Phil 2:6-8). He never used His miraculous birth as a "proof" and never once in the Gospels even mentions it Himself. And when He was hanging on the Cross, abandoned by everyone and in terrible agony, His accusers mocked Him precisely by requesting a miracle: "...come down now from the cross that we may see and believe " (Mk 15: 32). But He did not come down and they did not believe. Others, however, believed because of the fact that he did not come down from the cross, for they could sense the full divinity, the boundless height of that humility, of that total forgiveness radiating from the Cross: "Father, forgive them; for they know not what they do" (Lk 23:34). Once again, the Gospels and genuine Christian faith do not view miracles as proofs to force belief, since this would deprive man of what Christianity regards as most precious, his freedom. Christ wants people to believe in

Him willingly without the coercion of a miracle. "If you love me," Christ says, "you will keep my commandments" (Jn 14:15). And we love Christ—sadly, all too little—not because of His miracles and omnipotence, but because of His love, His humility and because, as those who heard Him said, "No man ever spoke like this Man!" (Jn 7:46).

All the same, Christ did perform miracles: the Gospels are full of stories about His healing the sick, raising the dead and so forth. Then what, we may ask, is the meaning of these miracles which Christ nevertheless chose to reveal to the world? If, according to the Gospels, He performed no miracles wherever people had no faith in Him, if He rebuked the people for expecting and looking for miracles from Him, then why did He do them? Only by answering this question can we perhaps understand the miracle of all miracles, the perpetual virginity of Mary His Mother, and the Church's unshakeable faith in this miracle. First, all the miracles we know from the Gospels were motivated by Christ's love. "He had compassion on them..." says the evangelist (Mt 9:36). He had compassion on parents whose young daughter had just died, on a widow who had lost her only son, on those who were celebrating and rejoicing at a marriage and did not have enough wine, on the blind, the lame, the suffering. What this means is that the miracle's source, once and for all, is love. Christ's miracles are performed not for Himself—for His own glorification, to reveal Himself and His Divinity and to prove it to people—but simply out of love. And because He loves, He cannot endure the suffering of a human being hopelessly imprisoned by evil.

Neverthless, this explanation still seems unrelated to

the miracle under discussion, Christ's birth from a Virgin, and her perpetual virginity. Indeed, this miracle is fundamentally unique, a mystery revealed and verified solely by our faith that Christ is God who because of His love became man and took upon Himself our humanity in order to save it. But to save it from what? From its total and inescapable slavery precisely to nature and those merciless laws which reduce us to just another species, just matter, just "flesh and blood." Man, however, is not merely of nature. Above all he is of God, of God's freely given love, of the Spirit. And therefore what our faith affirms is this: Christ is from God and of God, that His Father is God Himself. In Christ, in His birth, in His coming into the world a new humanity is born that comes not from the flesh nor from our self-imposed slavery to passions, but from God. God Himself is betrothed to humanity in the person of the most sublime fruit of His Creation: the all-pure Virgin Mary. And through her, through her faith and obedience, He gives us His only-begotten Son. The New Adam enters the world to be united with us and to lift up the first Adam who was created not "by nature" but by God. This is what we come to know, with trembling and joy, if we believe in Christ, and this is why when we accept Him as God and Savior, we recognize also His Mother's perpetual virginity through which the Spirit and Love conquer matter and its laws.

The Image of Woman

It is frightening and empty out in the world. Lonely. And infinitely difficult to live. This is why so many people are forever seeking some way out of this false and joyless life and get entangled in mind-numbing drunken-

ness, or in trying to out-swindle the swindlers and grab-
bing even the very slightest measure of simple animal
happiness, or in aimless dreaming. But sooner or later
these all come to a dead end and the forced march back to
the despised treadmill makes it all the more terrible. It is
no accident every aspect of life has today become "a
problem." The problem of society. The problem of work.
The problem of sex. The problem of woman. The problem
of happiness... Everything has become a problem because, on the one hand, the ready answers and prescrip-
tions of a corrupt system, long ago discredited and
stripped to their bare lies and emptiness, have ceased
being answers, and on the other hand, because no new
answers have taken their place, we often don't know how
and where to look. As a result our consciousness is con-
trolled by emptiness and cynicism, the very terrors we
wish to drown and escape.

Today, many people are hesitantly beginning to ac-
knowledge that genuine answers are impossible without
faith, without breaking through to what is transcendent
and eternal. But even faith in God takes different shapes
and can be merely some other way out, an escape, its own
brand of psychological drunkenness. In other words it
can be pseudo-faith, counterfeit faith. Sadly, it is possible
even in the name of faith and of God to hate and do evil,
to pull down and not build up. Christ himself said that
"many will come in my name...and lead many astray" (Mt
24:5), and "not everyone who says to me 'Lord, Lord'
shall enter the Kingdom of heaven" (Mt 7:21). Therefore,
from its very earliest days Christianity never simply
asked, "Do you believe?" for it knew that even Christ's
betrayers and crucifiers also had believed in something,

in some way. No, Christianity's question was this: How do you believe? And in what?

It is right here, in attempting to answer this question so fundamental to genuine faith, that the image of the Virgin Mother almost unconsciously and involuntarily begins to grow before our spiritual eyes. Oh, this doesn't mean that her image somehow eclipses the image of Christ, or that she is presented to Christianity as an additional object of faith set apart from Christ. Not at all, for it is from Christ and from Him alone that we receive this image as a gift, as the unfolding of all that His teaching and calling means. And so we ask ourselves, what is the strength of this image, what help does it give us?

My answer may surprise many people. What the Mother of God's image gives us first of all is the image of a woman. Christ's first gift to us, the first and most profound revelation of His teaching and call is given to us in the image of a woman. Why is this so important, so comforting and so redeeming? Precisely because our world has become so completely and hopelessly male, governed by pride and aggression, where all has been reduced to power and weapons of power, to production and weapons of production, to violence, to the refusal to willingly back down or make peace in anything or to keep one's mouth shut and plunge into the silent depths of life. The image of the Virgin Mary, the Virgin Mother, stands against all of this and indicts it by her presence alone: the image of infinite humility and purity, yet filled with beauty and strength; the image of love and the victory of love.

The Virgin Mary, the All-Pure Mother demands nothing and receives everything. She pursues nothing, and possesses all. In the image of the Virgin Mary we find what has almost completely been lost in our proud, aggressive, male world: compassion, tender-heartedness, care, trust, humility. We call her our Lady and the Queen of heaven and earth, and yet she calls herself "the handmaid of the Lord." She is not out to teach or prove anything, yet her presence alone, in its light and joy, takes away the anxiety of our imagined problems. It is as if we have been out on a long, weary, unsuccessful day of work and have finally come home, and once again all becomes clear and filled with that happiness beyond words which is the only true happiness. Christ said, "Do not be anxious... Seek first the Kingdom of God" (see Mt 6:33). Beholding this woman—Virgin, Mother, Intercessor—we begin to sense, to know not with our mind but with our heart, what it means to seek the Kingdom, to find it, and to live by it.

The Nativity of the Mother of God (September 8)

The Church's veneration of Mary has always been rooted in her obedience to God, her willing choice to accept a humanly impossible calling. The Orthodox Church has always emphasized Mary's connection to humanity and delighted in her as the best, purest, most sublime fruition of human history and of man's quest for God, for ultimate meaning, for the ultimate content of human life. If in Western Christianity veneration of Mary was centered upon her perpetual virginity, the heart of the Orthodox Christian East's devotion, contemplation, and joyful delight in Mary has always been her Motherhood, her flesh and blood connection to Jesus Christ. The East rejoices that the human role in the divine plan is pivotal.

The Son of God comes to earth, God appears in order to redeem the world, He becomes human to incorporate man into His Divine vocation, but humanity takes part in this. If it is understood that Christ's "co-nature" with us is Christianity's greatest joy and depth, that He is a genuine human being and not some phantom or bodiless apparition, that He is one of us and forever united to us through his humanity, then devotion to Mary also becomes understandable, for she is the one who gave Him His human nature, His flesh and blood. She is the one through whom Christ can always call Himself "The Son of Man."

Son of God, Son of Man... God descending and becoming man so that man could become divine, could become a partaker of the divine nature (2 Pet 1:4), or as the teachers of the Church expressed it, "deified." Precisely here, in this extraordinary revelation of man's authentic nature and calling, is the source of that gratitude and tenderness which cherishes Mary as our link to Christ and, in Him, to God. And nowhere is this reflected more clearly than in the Nativity of the Mother of God. Nothing about this event is mentioned anywhere in the Holy Scriptures. But why should there be? Is there anything remarkable, anything especially unique about the normal birth of a child, a birth like any other? And if the Church began to commemorate the event with a special feast it was not because the birth was somehow unique or miraculous or out of the ordinary; but because on the contrary, the very fact that it is routine discloses something fresh and radiant about everything we call "routine" and ordinary, it gives new depth to the "unremarkable" details of human life. What do we see in the icon of the feast when we look at it with our spiritual eyes? There on a bed lies a woman, Anna according to Church tradition, who has just given birth to a daughter. Next to her is the child's father, Joachim according to the same tradition. A few women stand by the bed washing the newborn baby for the first time. The most routine, unremarkable event. Or is it? Could it be that the Church is telling us through this icon that every birth, every entrance of a new human being into the world and life is a miracle of miracles, a miracle that explodes all routine, for it marks the start of something unending, the start of a unique, unrepeatable human life, the beginning of a new person. And with each birth the world is itself in some sense created anew and given as a gift to this new human being to be his life, his path, his creation.

This feast therefore is first a general celebration of Man's birth, and we no longer remember the anguish, as the Gospel says, "for joy that a human being is born into the world" (Jn 16:21). Secondly, we now know whose particular birth, whose coming we celebrate: Mary's. We know the uniqueness, the beauty, the grace of precisely this child, her destiny, her meaning for us and for the whole world. And thirdly, we celebrate all who prepared the way for Mary, who contributed to her inheritance of grace and beauty. Today, many people speak of heredity, but only in a negative, enslaving and deterministic sense. The Church believes also in a positive spiritual heredity. How much faith, how much goodness, how many generations of people striving to live by what is high and holy were needed before the the tree of human history could bring forth such an exquisite and fragrant flower—the most pure Virgin and All Holy Mother! And therefore the feast of her Nativity is also a celebration of human history, a celebration of faith in man, a celebration of man. Sadly, the inheritance of evil is far more visible and better known. There is so much evil around us that this faith in man, in his freedom, in the possibility of handing down a radiant inheritance of goodness has almost evaporated and been replaced by cynicism and suspicion... This hostile cynicism and discouraging suspicion are precisely what seduce us to distance ourselves from the Church when it celebrates with such joy and faith this birth of a little girl in whom are concentrated all the goodness, spiritual beauty, harmony and perfection that are the elements of genuine human nature. In and through this new-born girl, Christ—our gift from God, our meeting and encounter with Him—comes to embrace the world. Thus, in celebrating Mary's birth we find ourselves already on the road to Bethlehem, moving toward to the joyful mystery of Mary as the Mother to God

The Entrance of the Mother of God into the Temple (November 21)

It seems thousands of years removed from us, but it was not so very long ago that life was marked out by religious feasts. Although everyone went to church, not everyone, of course, knew the exact contents of each celebration. For many, perhaps even the majority, the feast was above all an opportunity to get a good sleep, eat well, drink and relax. And nevertheless, I think that each person felt, if not fully consciously, that something transcendent and radiant broke into life with each feast, bringing an encounter with a world of different realities, a reminder of something forgotten, of something drowned out by the routine, emptiness and weariness of daily life.

Consider the very names of the feasts: Entrance into the Temple, Nativity, Epiphany, Presentation, Transfiguration. These words alone, in their solemnity, their unrelatedness to daily life and their mysterious beauty awakened some forgotten memory, invited, pointed to something. The feast was a kind of longing sigh for a lost but beckoning beauty, a sigh for some other way of living.

Our modern world, however, has become monotonous and feastless. Even our secular holidays are unable to hide this settling ash of sadness and hopelessness, for the essence of celebration is this breaking in, this experience of being caught up into a different reality, into a world of spiritual beauty and light. If, however, this reality does not exist, if fundamentally there is nothing to celebrate, then no manner of artificial uplift will be capable of creating a feast.

Here we have the feast of the Entrance of the Mother of God into the Temple. Its subject is very simple: a little girl is brought by her parents to the temple in Jerusalem. There is nothing particularly remarkable about this, since at that time it was a generally accepted custom and many parents brought their children to the temple as a sign of bringing them into contact with God, of giving their lives ultimate purpose and meaning, of illumining them from within through the light of higher experience.

But on this occasion, as the service for the day recounts, they lead the child to the "Holy of Holies," to the place where no one except the priests are allowed to go, the mystical inner sanctum of the temple. The girl's name is Mary. She is the future mother of Jesus Christ, the one through whom, as Christians believe, God himself came into the world to join the human race, to share its life and reveal its divine content. Are these just fairy tales? Or is something given to us and disclosed here, something directly related to our life, which perhaps cannot be expressed in everyday human speech?

Here was this magnificent, massive, solemn temple, the glory of Jerusalem. And for centuries it was only there, behind those heavy walls, that a person could come into contact with God. Now, however, the priest takes Mary by the hand, leads her into the most sacred part of the Temple and we sing that "The most pure Temple of the Savior is led into the temple of the Lord." Later in the Gospels Christ said, "destroy this temple and in three days I will raise it up," but as the Evangelist added, "he spoke of the temple of His Body" (Jn 2:19, 21).

The meaning of all these events, words and recollections is simple: from now on man himself becomes the temple. No stone temple, no altar, but man—his soul, body and life—is the sacred and divine heart of the world, its "holy of holies." One temple, Mary—living and human—is led into a temple made of stone, and from within brings to completion its significance and meaning.

With this event religion, and life even more so, undergoes a complete shift in balance. What now enters the world is a teaching that puts nothing higher than man, for God himself takes on human form to reveal man's vocation and meaning as divine. From this moment onward man is free. Nothing stands over him, for the very world is his as a gift from God to fulfill his divine destiny.

From the moment the Virgin Mary entered "the holy of holies," life itself became the Temple. And when we celebrate her Entrance into the Temple, we celebrate man's divine meaning and the brightness of his high calling.

These cannot be washed away or uprooted from human memory.

The Annunciation (March 25)

The Annunciation! At one time, this was one of the brightest and most joyful days of the year, the feast which consciously, and even unconsciously, was connected with a jubilant intuition, a radiant vision of the world and of life. The Gospel of Luke records the story of the Annunciation.

> [The] angel Gabriel was sent from God to a city of Galilee named Nazareth, to a virgin betrothed to a man whose name was Joseph, of the house of David; and the virgin's name was Mary. And he came to her and said, "Rejoice, O favored one, the Lord is with you! Blessed are you among women!" But she was greatly troubled at the saying and considered in her mind what sort of greeting this might be. And the angel said to her, "Do not be afraid, Mary, for you have found favor with God. And behold, you will conceive in your womb and bear a son, and you shall call his name Jesus..." And Mary said to the angel, "How shall this be, since I have no husband?" And the angel said to her, "The Holy Spirit will come upon you, and the power of the Most High will overshadow you; therefore the child to be born will be called holy, the Son of God... For with God nothing will be impossible." And Mary said, "Behold, I am the handmaid of the Lord; let it be done to me according to your word." And the angel departed from her. (Lk 1:26-38)

Of course, viewed from the perspective of so-called "scientific" atheism this Gospel story supplies plenty of reasons for speaking of "myths and legends." The rationalist will say, "When do angels ever appear to young women and hold conversations with them? Do believers really think that people of the twentieth century, living in a technological civilization, could believe this? Can't believers see just how silly, unscientific and impossible this is?" The believer always has only one answer to this kind of contentious debate, disparagement and ridicule: yes, alas, it is impossible to fit this into your shallow worldview. As long as your arguments about God and religion remain on the superficial level of chemical experiments and mathematical formulas you will always easily win. But chemistry and mathematics are of no help whatsoever in proving or disproving anything at all in the realm of God and religion. In the language of your science, the words angel, glad tidings, joy and humility are of course completely meaningless. But why limit the discussion to religion? More than half of all words are incomprehensible to your rationalistic language, and therefore in addition to religion you will have to suppress all poetry, literature, philosophy and virtually the whole of human imagination. You desire the entire world to think as you do, in terms of production and economic forces, of collectives and programs. Yet the world does not naturally think in this way and must be handcuffed and forced to do so, or rather, appear to do so. You say that all imagination is false because the "imaginary" does not exist, and yet the imagination is what people have always lived by, live by now, and will in the future as well. For everything most profound and most essential in life has always been expressed in the language of imagination. I don't pretend to understand what an angel is, nor, using the limited language of rationalism, can I explain the event that occured almost two thousand years ago in a tiny Galilean town. But it strikes me that man-

kind has never forgotten this story, that these few verses
have repeatedly been incorporated into countless paint-
ings, poems and prayers, and that they have inspired and
continue to inspire. This means, of course, that people
heard something infinitely important to them in these
words, some truth which apparently could be expressed
in no other way than in the childish, joyful language of
Luke's Gospel. What is this truth? What happened when
the young woman, barely past childhood, suddenly
heard—from what profound depth, from what transcendent height!—that wonderful greeting: "Rejoice!" For
that is indeed the angel's message to Mary: Rejoice!

The world is filled with countless books on struggle and
competition, each attempting to show that the road to happiness is hatred, and in none of them will you find the word
"joy." People don't even know what the word means. But
the very same joy announced by the angel remains a pulsat-
ing force, that still has power to startle and shake human
hearts. Go into a church on the eve of Annunciation. Stay,
wait through the long service as it slowly unfolds. Then the
moment comes when after the long wait, softly, with such
divinely exquisite beauty the choir begins to sing the familiar festal hymn, "With the voice of the Archangel, we cry to
You, O Pure One: Rejoice, O Full of Grace, the Lord is with
You!" Hundreds and hundreds of years have gone by, and
still, as we hear this invitation to rejoice, joy fills our heart
in a wave of warmth. But what is this joy about? Above all
we rejoice in the very presence of this woman herself,
whose face, whose image, is known throughout the world,
who gazes upon us from icons, and who became one of the
most sublime and purest figures of art and human imagination. We rejoice in her response to the angel, to her

faithfulness, purity, wholeness, to her total self-giving and boundless humility, all of which forever ring out in her words: "Behold, I am the handmaid of the Lord; let it be to me according to your word." Tell me, is anything in this world, in any of its rich and complex history, more sublime and more beautiful than this one human being? Mary, the Most Pure One, the One who is Full of Grace, is truly the One in whom, as the Church sings, "all Creation rejoices." The Church answers the lie about man, the lie that reduces him to earth and appetite, to baseness and brutality, the lie that says he is permanently enslaved to the immutable and impersonal laws of nature, by pointing to the image of Mary, the most-pure Mother of God, the One to whom, in the words of a Russian poet, "the outpouring of sweetest human tears from overflowing hearts" is offered in unending stream. The lie continues to pervade the world, but we rejoice because here, in the image of Mary, the lie is shown for what it is. We rejoice with delight and wonder, for this image is always with us as comfort and encouragement, as inspiration and help. We rejoice because in gazing at this image, it is so easy to believe in the heavenly beauty of the world and in man's heavenly, transcendent calling. The joy of Annunciation is about the angel's Glad Tidings, that the people had found grace with God and that soon, very soon, through her, through this totally unknown Galilean woman, God would begin to fulfill the mystery of the world's redemption. There would be no thunder and no fear in His presence, but He would come to her in the joy and fullness of childhood. Through her a Child will now be King: a Child, weak, defenseless, yet through Him all the powers of evil are to be forever stripped of power.

This is what we celebrate on the Annunciation and why the feast has always been, and remains, so joyful and radiant. But I repeat, none of this can be understood or expressed in the limited categories and language familiar to "scientific" atheism, which leads us to conclude that this approach willfully and arbitrarily has declared an entire dimension of human experience to be non-existent, unnecessary and dangerous, along with all the words and concepts used to express that experience. To debate this approach strictly on its own terms would be like first climbing down into a black underground pit where, because the sky can't be seen, its existence is denied. The sun can't be seen, and so there is no sun. All is dirty, repulsive, and dark, and so beauty is unknown and its existence denied. It is a place where joy is impossible, and so everyone is hostile and sad. But if you leave the pit and climb out, you suddenly find yourself in the midst of a resoundingly joyful church where once again you hear, "With the voice of the Archangel, we cry to You, O Pure One: Rejoice!"

The Second Day of Christmas
The Assembly in Honor of the Mother of God (December 26)

It may be said without exaggeration that the growth of the Church's veneration of the Virgin Mary, the Mother of God, developed like a great tree from a tiny seed, from first contemplating her at the manger in Bethlehem. On that absolutely unique night for Christians when Jesus Christ was born, the image of Mother and Child became, and forever remains, the most important, profound, and joyful image of our faith... All the feasts, prayers, and love the Church now addresses to the

Mother of God are rooted in the celebration of Christ's birth.

In ancient times, when the Church calendar had not yet evolved, the one feast devoted to the Virgin Mary was on the second day of Christmas, December 26, known by its ancient title as "The Assembly in Honor of the Most Holy Mother of God." Precisely here, in the Church's celebration of Christ's birth, in the prayers and hymns of Christmas, that we find the deepest layer of Christian reflection on the Mother of God, our relation to her, our understanding of her example, her person and her place in our religious life.

One theme or motif woven throughout the Christmas celebration is the Church's experience of Christ's Mother as the world's gift to God, as humanity's gift to the One who comes to the world, to man. One of the Christmas hymns asks, "What shall we offer You, O Christ, who for our sakes has appeared on earth as man?" And then comes the answer: "All Creation offers You thanks: the angels offer a hymn; the heavens, a star; the wise men, gifts; the shepherds, their wonder; the earth, its cave; the wilderness, a manger. And we offer You a Virgin Mother!"

The profound significance of this remarkable hymn is that the world and all creation do not merely thirst for union with God or wait for His coming: they prepare for it, so that it is precisely the meeting of God with man, in freedom and love, that is at the heart of Christian faith. The modern ear, shrivelled and dried by superficial rationalism, hears words such as these about heaven meeting God with the gift of a star, or about the earth bringing gifts of a cave and manger, as "mere" poetic metaphor—for poetry, "as everyone knows," has no "objective" meaning whatsoever and is completely unrelated to reality. What our rational mind cannot grasp is that which poetry, and perhaps it alone, is capable of seeing, hearing, giving and revealing to us: the deepest meaning, or better, the inner depth to be found in every phenomenon, in every reality, that innermost core of power and truth hidden from the petty and self-satisfied rational mind occupied exclusively with externals. Heaven brings the star to Christ as a gift! This can only mean that everything, beginning with the world itself in all its wholeness and harmony, is naturally designed to reveal a higher meaning, that the world itself is no meaningless accident but on the contrary, is the symbol of God, the longing for God, the anticipation of God.

"The heavens are telling the glory of God!" (Ps 19:1). Poetry knows this, faith knows this. In Christ's birth, therefore, poetry and faith see not only that He comes into the world, but that the world goes out to meet Him: the star, the wilderness, the cave, the manger, the angels, the shepherds, the wise men. And at the radiant heart of this procession, as its center and fulfillment, stands Mary, the very best and most beautiful fruit of creation. It is as if faith says to God, "In Your love for us You give us Your Son; and we, in our love for You, give you Mary the Virgin Mother." In Mary the world is, so to speak, betrothed to God as the fulfillment of their mutual love. The Gospel says, "God so loved the world that He gave his only-begotten son..." (Jn 3:16); the Church answers: "The world so loved God that it gave Him the one whose beauty and purity reveal the world's deepest meaning and content..." The Son of God becomes through her the Son of Man, one of us, to make us one with Himself and through Him, one with

God. And therefore, before faith came to know Mary as Mother and intercessor, before veneration of Mary had fully matured into countless prayers, feasts and icons, what was first revealed as the foundation and source of all that followed was the Divine fulness and beauty of Christmas night. And at the heart of Christmas night is the image of Mother and Child streaming with blinding light. Here, everything that had been torn apart by sin and hostility and human pride is once again united: heaven and earth, God and man, nature and spirit. The world becomes a hymn of praise, words become a song of love, matter becomes a gift and all of nature becomes a manger. In this image of Mother and Child, God's eternal love for the world and the world's eternal love—in its inmost being—for God are united, completed and victorious. And this image no one has ever been able to uproot from human memory or consciousness.

Gazing at this image and rejoicing in it, we behold the only authentic image of the true world, of true life, of the true human being. And in blessing the Virgin Mother, we rejoice above all in what she reveals about ourselves and about the world's divine depth, beauty, wisdom and light when they are united with their loving Creator.

The Protection of the Mother of God (October 1)

This autumn celebration of the Mother of God's Protection became especially beloved among Russians, although the feast originated not in Russia but in Constantinople and, as strange as this may seem today, as a Byzantine victory celebration over the Slavic people who had besieged the capital city. According to tradition, people praying in Church during the siege suddenly saw the Mother of God praying for the city and holding her veil over it in protection. Later, as happened more than once in history, this limited local event outgrew the confines of its initial circumstances and acquired universal scope and meaning. The feast now has lost its link to history, and the specific details of its origin are largely forgotten, but what remains is the image of a Mother protecting, covering and comforting her afflicted children.

This feast became the heart of that experience of Mary as Mother, of the one who at the Cross was given to all humanity as Mother (see Jn 19:27), and who as Mother brings into her own heart all our sorrows, all our sufferings, all unbearable pain of our earthly existence. "A sword will pierce through your soul also, that thoughts out of many hearts may be revealed" (Lk 2:35). These words, prophetically spoken to her by the righteous Elder Simeon on the day she brought the Child into the Temple to consecrate Him to God, have deeply penetrated the souls of the faithful. The mother of Jesus Christ, standing at the Cross of her Son and taking upon herself all the terrible pain of compassion and co-suffering, became a gift to us, to humanity, a gift of maternal love, maternal care, maternal compassion...

For centuries people could sense and could spiritually see Mary's veil held out in protection over the world, and they rejoiced and found help and comfort. As the Church sings, "Today your faithful people brighly celebrate, blessed by Your appearance to us, O Mother of God." The first to see this vision of the Protection was St Andrew the Poor, the Fool-for-Christ, who told everyone that he had seen the Mother of God weeping for the world. "The Mother of God," he said, "was on her knees praying. The Lady and Queen of the world was weeping for it..."

Many centuries later, the great Russian philosopher and theologian Fr Sergius Bulgakov was asked about the meaning of those tears. In his youth he himself had abandoned Christianity and turned to Marxism, but during the years of national insanity, when millions were renouncing their faith, he returned to the Father's home and became a witness to his nation's religious vocation. This is his response, in a sermon on the day of this feast.

The Mother of God prays and weeps not just a thousand years ago, but here and now, at every time and in every place until the end of time. Her veil protects not only those who were present then, but every human generation, the whole world, all of us sinners. The Mother of God's veil which blesses and saves shines brightly at all times even if our eyes are unworthy to see it. The Mother of God stands between heaven and earth. She intercedes for the world and offers our petitions before the altar of God's throne. She is love and compassion, mercy and care, intercessor and defender. She does not judge, but has compassion for everyone. Hers is not to be the righteous judge, or the judge of righteousness, but to intercede as a mother. And at her Son's awesome tribunal she intercedes on our behalf with the Righteous Judge to ask forgiveness.

The world's sins and sorrows wound the heart of the one who loves all, and she responds to malice and sin with love and tears; a sword pierces her heart even now. The Mother of God weeps for the world. What does this mystery mean? The world weeps for itself through her tears. Its suffering and sadness are hers, its tears are her tears. She is Mother! She is heart. She is the fertile soil that drinks in the water... If only human eyes could perceive the Mother of God's presence in the world, they would know what transfiguration is mysteriously taking place. If they could only see her tears, their cruel hearts would be shaken into warmth. For no heart is so frozen as to remain unmelted in the face of her loving care. To malice she responds with love. To sin, with tears. To abuse, with forgiveness, to reviling with blessing.

The world is not abandoned to its suffering, man is not alone in his grief. The Mother's heart, too, is wounded and broken, the Mother of God weeps with us. One day we will know whose heart we wound with our sins and by whose tears they are washed away...

The Russian people came to love the Protection of the Mother of God first revealed in far-off Constantinople. Yet it was not there, but here in this distant northern land that the Mother of God's blessing of the world was most joyfully praised and celebrated. The Russian nation's soul bowed down before this wonderful appearance, and churches in honor of the Protection were built all across our land as hearts and knees knelt before the Mother of God. And now too, as the nation undergoes great sorrow, our people bless themselves with her protecting Veil. In these afflictions and sorrows how could she not hear the groans and sighs, the weeping and lamentation?

We believe and we know, that here as well the Compassionate One intercedes with prayer and tears for Russia's grief. Does our heart hear her crying? Has it experienced her prayer and comfort? Does it recognize her veil protecting our nation? Yes, whenever our heart bows in prayer before the All Pure One it hears her and knows her. While she does not resist its satanic trials, She has not abandoned our land.

Fr Sergius gave this sermon at the very start of the godless, antireligious madness that came over the Russian land, yet even today these words have not lost any of their power. For whatever new outward forms this battle may take, it remains a battle for the heart—the nation's, as well as the individual's—for the heart's direction, commitment and loyalty.

"Rejoice, O our joy! Protect us from all evil with your holy Veil." Our spiritual destiny was at one time defined by this exclamation of praise and joy, this prayer for help, protection and comfort. And no matter how many sins and falls there are, no matter how terrible life's darkness becomes, this radiant image of the Mother as intercessor, as comfort, as the world's protecting veil, has been with us, over us and within us... The feast of the Protection once again calls us to return, and in it to find healing and new birth.

The Dormition of the Mother of God (August 15)

In August the Church celebrates the end of Mary's earthly life, her death, known as her Falling Asleep or Dormition, a word in which dream, blessedness, peace, calm and joy are all united.

We know nothing of the circumstances surrounding the death of Mary, Jesus Christ's mother. Various stories, embellished with childlike love and tenderness, have come down to us from early Christianity, but precisely because of their variety we are under no compulsion to defend the "historicity" of any one of them. On Dormition the Church's commemoration and love are centered not on the historical and factual context, not on the date and place where this singular woman, this Mother of all mothers completed her earthly life. Wherever and whenever it occured, the Church looks instead at the essence and meaning of her death, commemorating the death of the one whose Son, according to our faith, conquered death, was raised from the dead and promised us final resurrection and the victory of undying life.

Her death is best explained through the Dormition icon placed in the center of the Church on that day as the focus of the entire celebration. The Mother of God has died and lies on her deathbed. Christ's apostles have gathered around her, and above her stands Christ himself, holding His Mother in His arms, where she is alive and eternally united with Him. Here we see both death and what has already come to pass in this particular death: not rupture, but union; not sorrow, but joy; and most profoundly, not death, but life. "After giving birth you remained a Virgin and after falling asleep you remained alive," sings the Church, gazing at this icon. "In giving birth you preserved your virginity, in falling asleep you did not forsake the world..."

The words of one of the deepest and most beautiful prayers addressed to Mary now come to mind, "Rejoice, bright dawn of the mystical Day!" (Akathist Hymn). The light which pours from Dormition comes precisely from that never-ending, mystical Day. In contemplating this death and standing at this deathbed we understand that death is no more, that a person's very act of dying has now become an act of living, the entrance into a larger life, where life reigns. She who gave herself completely to Christ, who loved him to the end, is met by Him at these radiant gates of death, and there at once death is turned into joyful meeting—life is triumphant, joy and love rule over all.

For centuries the Church has looked upon, reflected on and been inspired by the death of the One who was the mother of Jesus, who gave life to our Savior and Lord, who gave herself totally to Him to the very end and stood by Him at the Cross. And in contemplating her death the Church discovered and experienced death as neither fear, nor horror, nor finality, but radiant and authentic Resurrection joy. "What spiritual songs shall we now offer you, O most holy? For by your deathless Dormition you have sanctified the whole world..." Here, in one of the first hymns of the feast we immediately find expressed the very essence of its joy: "Deathless Dormition," deathless death. But what is the meaning of this contradictory, apparently absurd conjunction of words? In the Dormition, the whole joyful mystery of this death is revealed to us and becomes our joy, for Mary the Virgin Mother is one of us. If death is the horror and grief of separation, of descent into terrible loneliness and darkness, then none of this is present in the death of the Virgin Mary, since her death, like her entire life, is all encounter, all love, all continuous movement toward the unfading, never-setting light of eternity and entrance into it. "Perfect love casts out fear," says John the Theologian, the apostle of love (1 Jn 4:18). And therefore there is no fear in the deathless falling asleep of the Virgin Mary. Here, death is conquered from within, freed from all that fills it with horror and hopelessness. Death itself becomes triumphant life. Death becomes the "bright dawn of the mystical Day." Thus, the feast has no sadness, no funeral dirges, no grief, but only light and joy. It's as if in approaching the door of our inevitable death, we should suddenly find it flung open, with light pouring from the approaching victory, from the approaching reign of God's Kingdom.

In the glow of this incomparable festal light, in these August days as the natural world reaches the peak of its beauty and becomes a hymn of praise and hope and the ensign of another world, the words of Dormition ring out, "Neither the tomb nor death could hold the Mother of God, who is ever watchful in prayer, in whose intercession lies unfailing hope. For as the Mother of Life she has been transported to life..." Death is no longer death. Death radiates with eternity and immortality. Death is not rupture but union. Not sorrow but joy. Not defeat, but victory. This then is what we celebrate on the day of the Dormition of the Most Pure Mother, as we anticipate, taste and delight even now in the dawn of the mystical and never-ending Day.

2

Mary: The Archetype of Mankind

I

Virtually all Christian doctrines—the precise, conceptual formulation of the Church's faith and experience—developed as a response and reaction to various mutilations and distortions of that faith, to *heresies* in the literal meaning of the Greek word "airesis"—choice, i.e., reduction; therefore, deformation. Hence, one of the best ways to recover the essential meaning of this or that particular doctrine is to see it precisely in relation to the "heresy" it denounced, the question it answered.

We live today in a world full of "heresies": arbitrary choices and arbitrary reductions. Not only is it truly a broken world, with a broken vision and a broken knowledge, but its deep tragedy lies in this: that each "fragment" resulting from that brokenness is affirmed and experienced as the *whole* truth, each "reduction" is announced as "wholeness." Of this tragic reductionism Christians are more guilty than anyone else; for instead of healing it by the light and the power of the *catholic*, i.e., precisely whole, all-embracing and total vision, they themselves—for the sake of a superficial "relevance"—so often surrender to partial and broken "reductions" of "this world."

The best example here is precisely Mariology. While

Originally published in *The Univertsity of Dayton Review* (vol. 2, no. 3, 1975). Reprinted by permission.

some Christians make of it the very symbol of their staunch "conservatism" and live in the nostalgia of its medieval splendor, many others, indeed the majority, quietly abandon it as something precisely "medieval," "archaic," and therefore non-essential for what they want to be a new encounter of Christianity with the "modern" world. And they do it because they do not ask: to what eternal question is the Mariological experience of the Church the answer; of what basic—explicit or implicit— *heresy* is it the overcoming and the refutation? Yet only if we are able to rediscover in our knowledge and veneration of Mary that which is precisely *essential*, and this means that without which our Christian vision ceased to be *catholic*, becomes distorted, obscured, mutilated, only if, in other words, we learn how to relate Mariology to the fullness of Christian faith can we make ours again the true meaning of the Church's Mariological experience.

II

All I can do in this short paper is outline briefly, without either "proving" or developing it, the very general perspective in which, in my opinion, the rich Mariological tradition of the Church ought to be studied and understood today in our spiritually broken world.

It seems to me that the first task here consists in determining precisely that "heresy" to which the Christian answer is revealed in Mariology, although this answer itself obviously transcends the question and ultimately transforms its very nature. I have no doubt that this "heresy" concerns man and human nature, and that the essential theological context for the proper understanding of the Church's veneration of Mary is above all *anthropological*. This was true centuries ago when Mariology began to develop in its doctrinal aspects; this is especially true today.

Indeed the fundamental spiritual disease of our time, if one looks at it from a Christian standpoint, must be termed *anthropological heresy*. Its root is a deeply distorted understanding by man of his own nature and life. The most amazing, truly paradoxical aspect of that heresy, the aspect which strangely enough seems to be ignored by the defenders as well as the enemies of that heresy, is its fundamental inner contradiction, its being simultaneously an anthropological *minimalism* and an anthropological *maximalism*.

First, an anthropological *minimalism*. It is revealed and affirmed above all in the so-called human *sciences* whose entire emphasis lies precisely in the reduction of man to a phenomenon wholly determined by a network of impersonal natural laws of which man himself is but a result and "instrument." This reduction is studied and affirmed on many levels: the biological and genetic, the economic, the sociological, the psychological, but in all of them what is equally absent is precisely *freedom*, the possibility in man for a true personal self-determination. The old Feuerbachian definition, "man is what he eats," has been expanded so as to cover the entire "phenomenon of man," so as to become the basic "working hypothesis" in all possible approaches to that phenomenon.

At the same time, however, our culture is permeated with and truly based on an unprecedented *exaltation* of man, is the expression of an *anthropological maximalism* of proportions unknown in the past. The pathos of our "modern world" is the endless affirmation of man's absolute rights and freedom, the seeking of his *liberation* and *self-fulfillment*, the rejection of any limits to his "potential."

The amazing paradox of our culture, however, is that these two views of man, these two "anthropologies" so obviously excluding one another, are, in fact, "held together," constitute the fundamental worldview of the "modern man" who, in addition, seems to be totally unaware of its basic absurdity. The man is "nothing" yet he shall be "everything." There is no "freedom" in him, yet he is free. The person does not exist as a subject "transcending" its nature, but man has personal "rights." He is determined by his body but has the right truly to "dispose" of it. He has no "soul" but is an "absolute value..."

Had this paradox, this absurdity been confined to the area of mere theoretical speculation, it could easily be dismissed as a curious example of logical inconsistency. In reality, however, it is the very source of the present tragedy and predicament of man, of the apocalyptic flavor more and more evident in our culture. In Christian terms, it itself is precisely that *heresy* about man which, as all heresy, is above all an *existential*, and not merely theoretical, mutilation and distortion, resulting sooner or later in total chaos and total darkness. It is of this darkness that we have today the unmistakable foretaste... And the darkness is in this: that however *exalted* and *liberated*, i.e., "maximalized," man remains inescapably a slave of his own ontological "minimalism," a slave whose very dreams of happiness and self-fulfillment are—in the absolute sense of this world—*meaningless*.

It is this "broken anthropology," the source of all our tragedies and dead ends, that Christians ought to seek to heal today. And it is in Mariology, I am convinced, that they can discover the vision and the power necessary for that healing.

III

On the doctrinal level, Mariology, as is well known, began as the elucidation of the term *Theotokos*—the "Birthgiver of God," i.e., within the great Christological debate of the fourth and fifth centuries. This means that from the very beginning Mariology was understood as precisely an integral part of *Christology* and thus—ultimately—of the Christian experience of God and man. The term *Theotokos* which appeared at first within the *lex orandi*, i.e., as a liturgical term, was challenged as theologically absurd—How can God have a mother?—and misleading—Mary is the Mother of Christ and not of God. However, not only was that term maintained as liturgically permissible, it was moreover affirmed by the Church (Third Ecumenical Council: Ephesus, 431) as the adequate expression of the mystery of Incarnation, as an essential *epiphany* of its meaning. And although the Ephesus victory expressed itself in the liturgical veneration of Mary more than in theological speculation about her, it resulted in a vision of ineffable depth and beauty. It is this vision that we must decipher today, for—and this is my essential point—this vision contains and reveals precisely the *anthropological* expression and dimension of Christology; it is, so to speak, the fruit of Christology in anthropology.

Mariology developed in two simultaneous and, one should say, complementary movements. Both are not only possible, but equally essential and therefore necessary. The first one—the "Christological" proper—consists in explaining and experiencing the role of Mary in the Incarnation, the role which one can term instrumental. There can be no doubt that we have here the source and the essential basis of Mariology—that the latter begins with Christ, not with Mary "in herself." It is Christ, not Mary, who stands at the center of our faith, as its absolute content and power, fulness and joy. Yet—and this constitutes the second movement—looking at Mary's role in the Incarnation, at the "instrumentality" of that role, we unavoidably receive the revelation of Mary *herself*, and our knowledge *about* Mary is fulfilled as our knowledge of *her*. Because the "instrument" is revealed to us as a *person*, it is the person that gives the ultimate meaning of the "instrument." I am convinced that both aspects, both dimensions which together constitute, in a marvelous and beautiful synthesis, the very essence of the Church's veneration of the *Theotokos*, are essential for the Christian understanding of man, and contain the fundamental presuppositions of a truly Christian anthropology.

IV

There are those who think—and today more than ever—that the theological investigation of Mariology should not extend beyond the study of its "instrumental" aspect. We are concerned with Mary only inasmuch as she is the "instrument" of Christ's assuming human nature. Such seems to be their standpoint. They would accept Mariological devotion, but precisely as devotion, without seeking its significance for theology. What they do not seem to understand is that by setting such a limit, by drawing a line between theology and "devotion," they transform the latter into a virtually autonomous area, make Mariology into an almost independent "cult," whose dangers and exaggerations have been properly denounced in recent years. They do not see that if Mary is an essential part of the answer to the essential question, "Who is Christ?" this answer in turn concerns the other essential question, "Who is Mary?"—and, therefore, *who* and *what* is the human being itself. But perhaps it is by referring the totality of Mariology to the anthropological "heresy" mentioned above that we can see the importance of both *movements* within the Christian faith, the fundamental Christian "worldview."

Paradoxical as it may sound, Mariology in its first aspect—the "instrumental" one—supplies the "minimalistic" dimension of the modern view of man with a certain theological justification. At least it helps us to understand the anthropological minimalism as *verité chrétienne devenue folle* (a "Christian truth gone astray") and thus to restore it as the partial truth it certainly contains and implies.

Challenged with the modern exaltation of man and of his boundless "freedom," Christianity would stress, as does modern science, that man not only is part of "nature," but a part truly depending on nature, fundamentally subordinated to its "laws." There exists thus a certain parallel between the scientific view of man, in which the main category is that of dependence, and the theological, biblical view of man stressing his total dependence on God, the Creator of the world, of "nature" and of its "laws." There is also a convergence here in seeing the man as an "instrument," be it of a natural process or of God's design and plan. Just as science requests from man "obedience" to the objective laws of nature, the Bible and the Christian faith begin with an "unconditional surrender" of man to God, with total obedience and humility.

Is there any need to prove that in the economy of

Christian faith Mary stands, first of all, as the ultimate expression of that fundamental humanity and obedience to God's will and this means to "nature" itself which ultimately is the "instrument" of that Divine will and design? This, incidentally, is one of the main reasons for Mary's "rejection" by many "modern" Christians: she can hardly be construed as the symbol of that "liberation" which stresses the absolute "right" of man to dispose of his life and of his body in a manner which he himself chooses, to a "self-fulfillment" which he himself determines.

Thus, not only "science" but also "religion" begins with a certain "anthropological minimalism" with the recognition of a certain *limitation* of man, with his acceptance of God and a divinely established order and nature. And Mary, the "doule kyrion"—the "slave of the Lord" (Lk 1:38)—stands in the very center of the Church's vision of the world, of man and life as the ultimate fruit and therefore the highest expression of that "enslavement," humility and obedience, without which there is no entrance into the mystery of man's true communion with God.

But we part our ways with anthropological "minimalism" once we shift our attention from the first—instrumental—aspect of Mariology to the second one—to Mary as she is herself revealed in the mystery of the Incarnation and in the experience of the Church. For what we discover here is again the root, the initial inspiration, yet this time of anthropological "maximalism," which as we have seen, constitutes the second pole of the modern world view. We discover it as another "Christian truth gone astray."

Indeed what in the revelation of Mary—in the Gospel and then in the faith and the Tradition of the Church—is truly crucial, stands at its very center, and inspires the veneration of Mary with awesome amazement and endless joy, is another *dependence*: the dependence this time of the Incarnation itself, of the Divine plan itself, on the free and personal choice of Mary, on her free acceptance of the Divine challenge. The Divine plan and therefore "nature" are revealed as focused in a free person, i.e., a person capable of transcending all limitations, of revealing "nature" itself as fulfilling itself in freedom. Salvation is no longer the operation of rescuing an ontologically inferior and passive being; it is revealed as truly a *synergeia*, a cooperation between God and man. In Mary, obedience and humility are shown as rooted not in any "deficiency" of nature, aware of its own "limitations," but as the very expression of man's royal freedom, of his capacity freely to encounter Truth itself and freely to receive it. In the faith and the experience of the Church, Mary truly is the very icon of "anthropological maximalism," its eternal *epiphany*.

V

Properly understood, Mariology is thus the "locus theologicus" *par excellence* of Christian anthropology. In this unique knowledge of an unique Person, a knowledge which the Church always renews in her veneration of Mary, in communion with her and in joy about her, there can be dissolved the hopeless contradiction proper to the secular anthropology of our time: the contradiction between the "minimalistic" view of man stemming from science, and the "maximalistic" claims permeating our man-centered culture. What this personal knowledge and

contemplation of Mary reveals in a manner in which no
science, no theory, and probably even no "theology" as
such can reveal, is precisely the tragic falsehood of both
reductions—the "minimalistic" and the "maximalistic"—in their mutual alienation from one another, in their
hopeless "brokenness"; yet also the hidden truth of both
of them once they are integrated into that *wholeness*
whose only bearer and focus in the world is the human
person. What an abstract, i.e., impersonal, study of man
posits as its self-evident conclusion: man as total dependence; what an equally abstract "exaltation" of man posits
as its *a priori* premise: man as total *freedom*—are revealed in the unique *personal* experience of Mary, experience *given* to the Church and made into her experience,
as one and the same truth about man. In Mary, the very
notions of "dependence" and "freedom" cease to be op-
posed to one another as mutually exclusive. We are in-
clined to think that where there is dependence there can
be no freedom, where there is freedom there can be no
dependence. She, however, accepts, she obeys, she hum-
bles herself before—not her "dependence" on something
or somebody—but the living Truth itself, a Presence, a
Beauty, a Life, a Call so overwhelmingly evident that it
makes the notion of "dependence" an empty one, or
rather identical and coextensive with that of "freedom."
For as long as "freedom" is nothing but the "other side"
of dependence: as a protest, a rebellion against dependence; in other words, as long as "freedom" itself depends
on a dependence for its meaning—it is also an empty
notion: each time it "chooses" and "accepts" it ceases
to be freedom... Here, however, in the unique experience of
Mary, "freedom" becomes the very *content* of "depend-

ence," the one eternally fulfilling itself in the other as life, joy, knowledge, communion and fullness.

VI

These are poor, inadequate and clumsy human words about an experience, a vision, a reality which transcends all human words. But, having read them, look again at the Woman who eternally stands at the very heart of the Church, filling our hearts with a mysterious yet ineffable joy, making us repeat eternally that same salutation which she heard in the depth of her heart on the day of Annunciation: Rejoice! What is this joy about? Is it not about the revelation given us in her and through her and which—we know it—concerns each one of us and all of us, and which we tried, only tried, to indicate however poorly and inadequately in this paper? Truly she is unique because unique is her human perfection and unique her relation to her Son. And yet she is one of us, she is like us: her life, her experience are fully human. But then is it not in her and in her experience that we should seek the true "measure" of our own lives, the answer to the agonizing questions about man? Where else? Where else is the end and the solution of all the dichotomies and dead ends that threaten to dehumanize our world? She gave Christ to us. And He, who eternally remains her Son, gives her to us as the assurance that man is the image of His ineffable beauty, the object of an eternal love in an eternal Kingdom.

3

On Mariology in Orthodoxy

I

I am fully aware of the fact that the problem of Mariology does not seem to be central in Christian preoccupations today. I refer not only to non-Mariological churches, but even to Christians belonging to churches that were over-Mariological at times. When I attended Vatican II as an observer, a *peritus* said to me, "Well, we'll get rid of Mariology very soon." I still remember the shock I experienced then. In all honesty, we Orthodox are not ready to "get rid" of Mariology. On the contrary, I think that if we understood the crisis in which we find ourselves today, if we truly understood the depth of today's problems, and that the real crisis is on the level not of "adjustments" between the Church and the world (relevance!) but on that of the ultimate Christian vision of God, world and man, then we also would have understood what for centuries was expressed in the veneration of Mary.

I realize that it is difficult to see the connection between our "modern problems" and Mary, because in the Catholic West she has become the object of an almost separate cult. In the East, on the other hand, she is "taken for granted" and provokes no theological questioning or reflection. There is no "Mariology" in the Orthodox Church if this term is taken to mean a specific theological

Originally printed in *Marian Library Studies* (vol. 2, 1970). Reprinted by permission.

discipline, a separate intellectual set of problems. The veneration of Mary permeates, so to speak, the entire life of the Church; it is a "dimension" of dogma as well as piety, of Christology as well as ecclesiology. It is this "dimension" that is to be made explicit today, and in connection mostly with the problems that seem so alien to it. In other words, one is to ask the question: Is Mariology a type of piety relevant in the past but no longer of value today? My preliminary answer is no. Something is expressed in Mariology which is fundamental to the Christian faith itself, to the Christian experience of the world and of human life. It is in this area that I will try to share some thoughts with you.

II

Although I will not discuss the historical development of Mariology, I must stress that the Orthodox understanding of it has always been in "Christological terms." To use a somewhat paradoxical approach, I would say that if nothing else were revealed in the Gospel than the mere fact of Mary's existence, i.e., that Christ, God and man, had a mother and that her name was Mary, it would have enough for the Church to love her, to think of her relationship with her Son, and to draw theological conclusions from this contemplation. Thus, there is no need for additional or special revelations; Mary is a self-evident and essential "dimension" of the Gospel itself.

As to liturgical veneration, Mariology developed at first within the frame-work of the so called "concomitant feasts." The oldest feast of Mary seems to have been the "Synaxis" in her honor on December 26, immediately following the Nativity. This means that liturgical veneration of Mary followed the development of Christology; it was a part of the Church's contemplation of the mystery of the Incarnation. In the East at least, this Christological character of the veneration of Mary has always been preserved. We have, of course, popular forms of Marian devotion, but even these remain organically connected with the mystery of Christ. And this remains the inner norm and criterion of Orthodox Mariology.

The liturgy is the main, if not exclusive, *locus* of Mariology in the Orthodox Church. As I said before, Mary has never become the object of any special and separate theological speculation; one would seek in vain for a Mariological treatise in our manuals of dogma. This liturgical veneration has, to be sure, been adorned with much piety, symbolism and allegory, and this has led to questions about the biblical character and justification of these forms. Where in the Bible do we find stories about her nativity, her presentation in the Temple, her dormition—all of the principal Mariological celebrations. To this the Orthodox answer is that whatever their poetic, liturgical and hymnographic "expressions," all these events are *real* in the sense that they are self-evident. Mary was born; as with every pious Jewish girl she was, at some moment of her life, taken into the Temple; and, in the end, she died. The fact, therefore, that much of the liturgical expression of these feasts is taken from the Apocrypha does not change or alter their "reality." It is the ultimate meaning of these events that the Church contemplates, not the poetic elaborations of Byzantine hymns.

Mariological feasts are only one aspect of the veneration of Mary. Indeed, it permeates the entire worship of the Church. Thus, we find her veneration at the end of each liturgical unit, as its conclusion or epilogue. Each group of hymns or prayers is always concluded with the *Theotokion*, a special hymn to Mary. On Wednesdays and Fridays, days dedicated to the Cross, this prayer takes the form of a *Stavrotheotokion*, a hymn in which Mary is contemplated standing at the Cross.

Finally, a very important dimension of Mariology is to be found in iconography. It is enough, for example, to look at one of the best Marian icons of the Orthodox East—*Our Lady of Vladimir*—to understand that herein there is a wonderful revelation about the central mystery of the Christian faith, as well as the meaning of man, his body, his life, his destiny.

III

But this is being challenged today; an attempt to explain becomes inevitable. Such an explanation must of necessity "desiccate" an organic whole and show its different strata. In the first place, we find the very important theme of Mary as the *New Eve*. It can be termed the "cosmological" aspect of Mariology. At the same time it sets the framework for the entire mystery: the relationship between God and the world (cosmology), God and his chosen people (history of salvation), God and the Church (ecclesiology) and finally, the consummation of all things in God. All this is expressed primarily as a mystery of love, in terms of marital unity. The second theme is that of *Mary as Temple*. It finds its ultimate expression in the feast of the Presentation of Mary in the Temple. The Temple is the place of Divine presence, of encounter between God and man, of the revelation of Divine glory. In this feast the ultimate mystery of man as the Temple of God is revealed to us. Mary represents all of us in this fulfillment of one Temple in and through the other—the human—Temple. Finally, the *death* of Mary, the great theme of Dormition. If I am permitted a word here by way of a friendly ecumenical critique, the Catholics should never have permitted their theologians to "elaborate" the mystery of the Assumption (as also that of the Immaculate Conception). They missed the whole point, for they tried to explain rationally—and in inappropriate terms—an eschatological mystery. The Orthodox Church does not "explain" what happened when Mary died. It simply states that her death signifies the "morning of a mysterious day," that Mary, in virtue of her total love for God and surrender to him, of her absolute obedience and humility, is the beginning of that common resurrection which Christ announced to the world.

Each of these themes requires a long and elaborate treatment. Here I will only touch upon one aspect of Mariology; its meaning for the doctrine and understanding of the Church.

IV

Ecclesiology is one of the great themes of our ecumenical age. And the first thing one must say about ecclesiology is that today it is "polarized." It is polarized between the notions of authority and freedom. One can say that the old presentations of *De Ecclesia* are coming to an end. As we know today, the classical *De Ecclesia* with its emphasis on structure, institution and legalism is the product of the confessional polemics, of the great Western crisis of Reformation-Counter-Reformation. It is this *institutional* or structural reduction of ecclesiology that is being challenged and denounced today. Yet, as it always happens, one extreme leads to another. When

people tire of "structures" and "institutions," they jump
into a kind of illusion of freedom, not realizing that in
shaking one set of structures, they prepare another one.
Today's freedom will become tomorrow's "institutions,"
and so on *ad infinitum*. Perhaps it is time for us to realize
that as long as we debate institutions and structures, and
not the mystery of the Church in her depth, we are by-
passing the real issue.

What is the Church? On the one hand the Church is
certainly structure and institution, order and hierarchy,
canons and chanceries. Yet this is only the visible structure. What is its content? Is it not also, and primarily, that
which is to change and to transfigure life itself? Is it not
the anticipation, the "Sacrament" of the kingdom of God?
Yes, the Church is structure, but the unique purpose of
that structure is to be an "epiphany," to manifest and to
fulfill the Church as expectation and fulfillment, as pilgrimage and anticipation. The Church is thirst and hun-
ger, and she is also the "food of immortality." She is the
"not yet" and the "already is..." Now, it is in this perspective—that of the Church as life, and not only structure—
that we can understand the unique place of Mary in "ecclesiology," i.e., the attempt to understand the Church
from within.

It is, of course, in worship that this experience of the
Church is given. It is in her *leitourgia* that the Church
transcends herself as institution and structure and becomes "that which she is": response, adoration, encounter, presence, glory, and, ultimately, a mystical marriage
between God and his new creation. It is precisely here
that Mary stands at the center—as the personification, as
the very expression, icon, and content of that response, as

the very depth of man's "yes" to God in Christ. In the worship of the Church there comes the moment when all structures *qua* structures disappear; they are fulfilled. They are essential, necessary to bring us up to that moment, to make that moment possible. Yet when it comes, it is life and life alone that triumphs. It is that perfect experience of unity and joy that is given—and here stands Mary as, indeed, the personal "icon" of the Church, of that movement of love and adoration.

There is no "icon" of the Church except the human person that has become totally transparent to the Holy Spirit, to the "joy and peace" of the Kingdom. If Christ is the "icon" of the Father, Mary is the "icon" of the new creation, the new Eve responding to the new Adam, fulfilling the mystery of love.

She is the New Eve because of God's request that she answered, "I am the servant of the Lord, be it done to me according to his word." At that moment all human "structures" which originated in man's alienation from God—freedom and authority, rights and obligations, etc.—all this was transcended. The new life entered the world as life of communion and love, not of "authority" and "submission." Thus, being the "icon" of the Church, Mary is the image and the personification of the world. When God looks at his creation, the "face" of the world is feminine, not masculine. We men are, to be sure, co-workers with God. We are the heads of families, churches, institutions, etc. We become bishops, priests, superintendents. Unfortunately, some women today think that they should also become priests and bishops. They are wrong, for when it comes to holiness and joy, to ultimate reality and transfiguration, it is the "feminine" qualities of humility, beauty, obedience and total self-giving that triumph in the "new creation" and crown it with Divine glory. It is symbolic indeed that on Mount Athos, the great monastic center of the Orthodox East, no woman is admitted. Yet, the whole mountain is considered to be the particular possession of the Mother of God. The intuition of the great Russian novels like *Anna Karenina* or *Dr Zhivago* is that in spite of all its ambiguity, its tragic identification with the demonic temptation, its deviation from the Divine beauty, it is here, in the mystery of woman that the last word of creation is to be revealed. She—Mary—is the ultimate "doxa" of creation, its response to God. She is the climax, the personification, the affirmation of the ultimate destiny of all creation: that God may finally be all in all, may fill all things with himself. The world is the "receptacle" of his glory, and in this it is "feminine." And in the present "era," Mary is the sign, the guarantee that this is so, that in its mystical depth the world is already achieving this destiny.

Our world today is "masculine" in the sense that it concentrates almost everything on forms and structures, on institutions and categories, but not on the content in which these structures exist and which is their final justification. This "masculine" approach has contaminated theology itself. But the "epiphany" of the Church always takes place beyond the structures, as their fulfillment. There comes a time when the institution disappears, although without the institution that moment would have never come, would have been impossible. This is when the Church is actualized as "joy and peace" in the Holy Spirit, is the taste—here and now—of the Kingdom which is to come. At the heart of that moment, as its expression, movement and perfection, we find Mary. She is not the "object" of prayer and adoration, but its very expression. She is the Church as prayer, as joy, as fulfillment. It is this combination of beauty and humility, matter and spirit, time and eternity, that is the real experience of the Church and of that experience Mary is the focus and the life. It is for this experience that the world is longing today.

We think that we can solve all problems today by "masculine" means—by changing institutions and adopting new laws, by planning and calculating. In the end, however, this alone cannot and will never triumph. What will always win while being defeated is something quite different: a vision, an experience which is behind all these structures and alone can give them significance, the victorious humility of the Church as personified in Mary. The Church should not adopt—as she seems to do today—a "me-too" attitude, that of simply joining the world in its struggles, protests, pickets, and in all "human, all too human" wisdom and passion. Throughout the centuries she has accumulated another wisdom, another experience, something for which every man and woman, every society and generation, is really nostalgic. For behind all the struggles and conflicts which fill the world, there is the secret, unknown and unconscious desire for the ultimate synthesis, a convincing image of man and manhood. This is what the Church, and she alone, can offer to the world.

This is what I call the Mariological dimension of ecclesiology. I do not find it discussed in modern theology. On the contrary, what we want to prove to ourselves and to the world is how "masculine," structured, and, in general, how "this-worldly" we are. We are indeed ashamed of Mariology, perceiving it as weakness and sentimental deviation. There must be someone, then, who in the midst of this surrender would simply affirm and proclaim the eternal validity of the Mariological "focus" of the Church. And if we take one by one the various problems which constitute the "agenda" of our times and study them in the light, not of superficial Mariology, but of its deep implications and insights, of the silent vision behind it, this may be, in spite of all theological inflation and the noise of our days, the best way to serve the world. We have received a gift from God and we can share it with the world, thirsty and hungry, in joy and beauty. Mary is the secret joy of all that the Church does in this world. It is she who can and will purify the world, not priest's unions and masses of protest. She will reveal to us that which we are losing every day, the *mysterium* of the Church, that without which everything in the Church loses all meaning. This is why the Mariological theme is actual. We have not yet started to work on it, but I would suggest that, instead of adding to the world's crowds of specialists in all possible areas, we return with a new interest to the one in whom God has given us both "icon" and "power" to become that which Christ wants us to be.

4

Mary and the Holy Spirit

I

The theme which I was asked to treat here today seems to me to be a very timely one, and this for two reasons. On the one hand, we witness today among Christians a certain renewal of the interest, both theological and spiritual, in the Holy Spirit. There is a feeling—however vague and confused at times—that the neat and rigid theologies of the past were in a way one-sided. They were aimed at justifying and explicating the "institutional" rather than the "spiritual" aspect of the Church. As a reaction to this, there appeared a new thirst for the spiritual reality itself; hence this renewed interest in the Holy Spirit. No doubt this interest, this preoccupation with the spiritual, is not free from the spiritual confusion typical of our time. One ascribes to the Holy Spirit almost any movement or even fantasy of man's mind and imagination; one justifies by Him all kinds of radicalisms and the pervasive "anti-institutionalism" of contemporary religious mentality. It is then the proper task for a theologian to ask the proper questions about the Holy Spirit.

On the other hand, and this is my second reason, there is an equally obvious decline in Mariological interest. Those who, in the past, seemed almost to exaggerate the place of Mary in the economy of salvation and in the piety of the Church, are today somewhat apologetic about

Originally printed in *Marian Studies* (vol. 23, 1972). Reprinted by permission.

this. In the enormous theological production generated by Vatican II, the Mother of God is hardly mentioned. It seems as if the new emphasis and concerns of theology, its obsession with notions such as "world," "relevance," "justice," etc., exclude, if not tacitly condemn, the previous emphasis on Christ's Mother. Strange as it may seem, even the very modern and fashionable interest in the woman's place in the Church, the world, and society, or the great wave of "feminism," has not revived Mariological interests. Certainly one can easily understand why! In her humility and silence, she can hardly serve as patron for the noisy and arrogant feminism of our time.

Now it is precisely this double phenomenon—a revival of pneumatology and a decline of Mariology—that calls for their joint investigation. We must study the unique relationship between the Third Person of the Blessed Trinity and the unique person whom we still venerate, and I hope shall venerate eternally, as "...more honorable than the Cherubim and beyond compare more glorious than the Seraphim..." I am convinced that pneumatology and Mariology are organically connected in the *experience* of the Church and therefore must be connected in her theology. If indeed it is the Holy Spirit who *reveals* Mary to us, it is Mary who in a unique way is the revelation in the Church of the Holy Spirit. I am further convinced that the contemporary and confused interest in the Holy Spirit, valuable and promising as it is, will not lead to His genuine rediscovery unless it becomes at the same time an interest in the most spiritual one; that the Mariological decline will not be overcome unless Mariology is no longer viewed as a devotional department of the Church, but is integrated into pneumatology.

II

At this point a few words are necessary on the fate of pneumatology in the history of Christian thought. One doesn't have to prove that in systematic theology the elaboration of pneumatology has always been much less emphasized than, let's say, Christology or several other aspects of the *depositum fidei*. As everyone knows, even in the universal creed of the Church the word "God" has been omitted for reasons of ecclesiastical diplomacy in the article concerning the Third Person. At a rather early date, the theology of the Holy Spirit was replaced in theological manuals with the theology of grace, a refined and detailed enumeration of all modes of sanctification. The Holy Spirit, to be sure, has never been denied the place which is His; formally, theology always remained trinitarian. Yet one cannot help thinking that something happened within the Christian society which shifted its attention, its love, its hope from that mysterious third hour, from those tongues of fire which manifested the descent of the Paraclete. It is impossible for me to analyze this "something" be it in a short way. I will simply state what I consider to be the reason for this theological eclipse of the Holy Spirit. It was a shift from the eschatological inspiration of the early Church—and by eschatological I mean here the unique Christian experience of the Kingdom of God, as, on the one hand the Kingdom "to come," and, on the other hand, as that same Kingdom present and actualized in Church. This eschatology in the early Church constituted the essential dimension of her entire life—sacraments, world, faith, piety—and shaped the entire mind of the Church; it was her attitude towards world, time, history, society, etc. This eschatology little by little was reduced to a brief theological chapter—"*de novissimis*"—dealing with the individual fate of man after death. The notions of the Kingdom, the consummation of all things in God, of the new creation and transfiguration, to be sure, remained part of the traditional vocabulary, but they ceased to be both the source and the object of theological elaboration.

Eschatology, however, is inseparable from pneumatology, for it is the coming of the Holy Spirit, it is Pentecost that inaugurates the "new eon" and makes the Church and the life in the Church both communion with, and anticipation of, the Kingdom of God. More than that, it is the very fellowship, communion, *koinonia* of the Holy Spirit, that is the very essence of the new life, of the Kingdom of God. It is He who makes all things new by referring them to the ultimate consummation of all things in God. Pentecost is not only the historical source of the Church; it is her very life as the sacrament of the Kingdom. All this is confusedly felt today by all those who are tired of the institutional and non-eschatological character emphasized so much throughout the long historical pilgrimage of the Church and who are thirsty and hungry for the spiritual reality itself. The danger here, however, is that of a new divorce, a new dichotomy: the "spiritual" versus the "institutional"; the Holy Spirit versus the Church; the individual subjectivity of the spiritual experience versus catholic faith and discipline. The danger is that one takes the Holy Spirit as a kind of *alibi* for mere dissent and rebellion, anarchy and subjectivism, so as to confuse eschatology with human radicalism and utopianism.

It is at this point, it seems to me, that the need for

Mariology becomes obvious. For, indeed, Mary, being in the tradition and experience of the Church the very "epiphany" of spirituality, being herself the first, the highest and the most perfect fruit of the Holy Spirit in the entire creation, reveals to us by her very presence the true nature and the true effects of the Descent of the Holy Spirit which is *the* source of the Church's life. To put it somewhat differently, Mariology, properly understood, is a kind of "criterion" for pneumatology, a safeguard against a demonic confusion of spirits. In this short paper I can only enumerate, without really explaining them, the various aspects of this unique relationship.

III

The relationship between the Holy Spirit and Mary is both *unique* and *archetypal*. It is unique in the sense that it reveals to us Mary as a unique human being, unique in herself as a person, unique in her relationship to Christ and to God, unique by her place in the Church, i.e., in her relationship to all of us and to each one of us. It is archetypal in the sense that it reveals the very nature of the Holy Spirit in His relationship with the creature, the true nature of what we call sanctification.

The story of Mary in the Gospel begins with her personal Pentecost. "The Holy Spirit shall come upon you" (Lk 1:35). Already here we begin to understand something about both the Holy Spirit and Mary. In the first place and above everything else, this descent of the Holy Spirit reveals a *personal* relationship. More than that, it *fulfills* Mary as a person; this means as an absolutely unique being, as totally *herself*. A certain type of theology and a certain type of piety went to extremes in stressing this uniqueness of Mary, and this at the expense of the archetypal character of her personal Pentecost. Yet it is precisely the proper function of the Holy Spirit to fulfill human beings as persons. He is to each one the very gift of uniqueness, of that uniqueness which constitutes the eternal and absolute value of each person. Thus, in the personal Pentecost of Mary, we have two revelations. It reveals God as always a unique and personal revelation to each one, as if each person sees in God a unique face turned to him in an exclusive relationship, unique love, and most personal communion. Thus, two gifts.

The gift of Mary as a person. In the Holy Spirit we know her, not as a symbol, not as a theological idea, not as a principle, or tool, or illustration; we know *her*! And to know her is one of the greatest joys available to man in the Church. If every friendship, every personal encounter, every communion, however limited, with another person is always experienced as a gift, as something enriching, as indeed the very context of life whereas solitude and loneliness is simply death, then what can we say about this unique friendship and communion which has been given to us in the Church by the Holy Spirit? What was this slow growth of the Mariological veneration in the Church if not the growth of that knowledge, friendship, communion? No formal theology can explain this because it deals with unchanging relations and definitions; it can only establish and define the framework and the context. But the content is in the life of the Church, in the mystery of her worship which is an unending growth. If one had to prove with one simple proof the ongoing presence and action of the Holy Spirit in the Church, I would point to Mariology, to this ever-growing knowledge of Mary as a person. It is as if living with her in the same house and sharing in the same life, we always discover more and more reasons to love her and to treasure her personality.

The second gift is the gift of the Holy Spirit Himself as God *for me* and *to me*, as both the content and the fulfiller, as the very life of my life. The Holy Spirit has no icon of His own; no name of His own. Yet, the sanctification consists precisely in this: that each being and even each thing becomes such an icon and such a name. It is by becoming transparent to the Holy Spirit, by reflecting His goodness and beauty, by becoming fully life in Him and truly His fragrance that beings become, on the one hand, fully themselves as persons and, on the other hand, truly the icons and the names of the Holy Spirit. Of this, Mary is indeed the first and the fullest epiphany. In this sense she is the first icon, the first gift, the first manifestation of the Holy Spirit. If He makes us to know her, she is the first in the entire creation to make us know Him. This is what makes Mariology the first and most important *locus* of pneumatology.

The Holy Spirit is then Giver of Life, of life not as a mere existence but as content, as a personal fulfillment by a unique being of its "nature." The life which the Holy Spirit gives to Mary in Christ. Her divine motherhood is not one single event among many in her existence, an event which, having taken place, leaves her, so to speak, available for other events and other fulfillments. It is the decisive and all-embracing event which consumes the totality of her being, yet at the same time, makes and fulfills that being for all eternity. She is "nothing else," but this "nothing else" is not a negative definition but indeed a most positive one: to have Christ and "nothing else" as one's life is the ultimate wholeness, the absolute fulfillment of humanity.

Thus, here again, we find revealed and given to us a double mystery, a double gift. On the one hand, this divine motherhood of Mary is a unique revelation of the Holy Spirit about her and about Christ. Their relationship is revealed to us as an object of eternal contemplation and joy, as that which makes us and is to make us rejoice eternally in the Kingdom of God. On the other hand, we have here the revelation of the new creation, and this means of the Church, and of the life of each one of us in the Church, as having Christ for its content and fulfillment—Christ and "nothing else." The gift of the Holy Spirit is thus a gift of wholeness. As Giver of Life, He gives to each one as his personal life and as his personal fulfillment the One in whom "was life and that life was the light of men" (Jn 1:4). By the Holy Spirit, Christ is unique to Mary as her Son, and therefore her life. But then Mary is truly the icon and the epiphany of the Church—of the Church as life in Christ and of the Church as Christ's life in us, of the Church as indeed wholeness.

If today we experience a painful divorce and a discrepancy between the "institutional" and the "spiritual" aspects of the Church—between the Church as structure, hierarchy, authority, dogma, and the Church as life, freedom, growth, beauty, joy—it is, I am convinced, because we have forgotten the reality in which this dichotomy is always transcended and overcome: the mystery of Mary whom the Holy Spirit makes the personal focus, icon and fulfillment of the Church. How truly sad and tragic are the modern attempts to rediscuss and redefine the Church in terms of sociological structures, and the poor human dichotomies of

authority and freedom, uniformity and pluralism, to reduce her to all that which Nietsche called "...human, all
too human." I am sure that the great ecclesiological crisis
of our time can find its solution only when we relate
again the mystery of the Church to the mystery of Mary,
and this means the mystery of the Holy Spirit.

The Holy Spirit comes "on the last and great day of
Pentecost." He is the Giver and the Revealer of the "last
things." He comes at the end, or rather, His coming, because
it reveals the "last things," is the fulfillment, is always the
end, the eschaton. The end, however, in the Christian faith
is the Kingdom of God, the fulfillment and consummation
of all things in God, the ultimate revelation of "the grace of
our Lord Jesus Christ, the love of God the Father, and the
communion of the Holy Spirit." The end is thus always the
beginning of all things made new. And the first revelation
of these "last things," of that consummation in God, the first
epiphany by the Holy Spirit of the reality of the Kingdom,
is *Mary*. If we know "something" about the Kingdom of
God, about what it means to be consummated in God, to be
deified, to be raised in glory, to be nothing but light, peace,
and joy, to be fully one's self and yet to be fully united to
God, to be "nothing else" and yet "everything," to be creation and yet to ascend to Heaven, immortal and full of life,
we know it first of all because in the Church we know Mary.
Without this "existential" knowledge, without her constant
presence in the Church as her prayer and beauty, movement
and peace, joy and fullness, all this would have remained
mere doctrinal "propositions," something that cannot be
existentially verified and truly appropriated not only as a
dogma but as, above all, experience and knowledge. Indeed,
it is not accidental that whenever and wherever Mariology

declines, and this means the veneration of Mary and the joy about Mary, there also declines the eschatological joy of the Christian faith. The Church begins to be viewed as an agency for social reform and worldly service, and "secularism" makes its triumphant, although sickening, entrance.

This "secular" Christianity of which we hear so much today is first of all a Christianity without the experience of the "last things," and this means without the Holy Spirit and without Mary. If we think that we can help the world (not even to speak of its salvation) by the boredom and the verbiage of our social and political pronouncements, of our miserable efforts to out-shout the secular professionals of all kinds of secular "liberations," we are, sooner or later, in for a terrible disillusion. For it is the Church's knowledge of the "last things" that is the only source for her *praxis* in the world. It is faith, hope and love stemming from that knowledge and from that experience that alone can teach the Church and each Christian what they are to do in this ever-changing world and its history. More than anything else, we need today a re-plunging, a re-immersion into the Church's experience of the eschaton. Any other knowledge is impossible without the Church and is her exclusive gift to the world. This immersion, however, will not be possible without the rediscovery of the eschatological dimensions of the mystery of Mary, without our learning to contemplate and experience in her the mystery of the Kingdom as revealed to us by the Holy Spirit.

IV

I have said enough, I hope, to show at least one thing: that pneumatology and Mariology, far from being two distinct and separate areas of Christian theology and experience are, on the contrary, connected with one another in a most organic and essential way. The proper study and understanding of one can never be full or even adequate without the other. If Mariology declines today, it is probably because for too long a time it was disconnected from pneumatology and began to be choked within itself by its own closed horizon. If the modern revival of the interest in the Holy Spirit, and, more generally, in the "spiritual," seems so often to orient itself at wrong directions and tragic and dangerous dead ends, it is probably because of its disconnection from the spiritual experience of the Church, experience at whose very center stands the Church's knowledge of Mary.

Today, more than ever, we are called to "test the spirits to see whether they are of God; for many false prophets have gone out into the world" (1 Jn 4:1). How are we to test them if not by the very faith and experience of the Church? More than ever, it is time for us to rediscover in the mystery of Mary a sure and inspiring criterion for such a test and joyfully to accept her as the greatest gift and revelation of the Holy Spirit.

5

Mary in Eastern Liturgy

A student of Mariology in the Orthodox Church may be struck by two apparently contradictory facts: on the one hand, a tremendous richness of Mariological material in liturgy, yet, on the other hand, a virtual absence of specifically Mariological studies in theology. It is indeed a real paradox of the Orthodox East that the whole of its Mariological experience and piety seems to have permeated its worship but did not provoke any significant theological reflection. We have nothing that would correspond to specialized Mariological treatises in the West, and in our manuals of dogmatics there are no separate chapters dealing with the place of Mary in the economy of salvation. Thus, the veneration of Mary—so obvious, so central in worship—has not been expressed, analyzed, or evaluated systematically.

At first this scarcity of theological reflection may appear to be a deficiency of Orthodox theology. How could it happen that the Church which never prays to God or Christ without at the same time addressing her prayers to Mary, which constantly praises the one who "...is more honorable than the cherubim and beyond compare more glorious than the seraphim..." has not directed its theological mind to this enormously important fact of its life

Originally printed in *Marian Studies* (vol. 19; 1968). Reprinted by permission.

and piety? Upon deeper investigation, however, one comes
to ask whether this absence of theological speculation is not
itself an integral part of the "mystery of Mary" in the
experience of the Church, whether theology as such—i.e.,
the rational investigation of the *depositum fidei*—is fully
adequate to transpose into its precise terms the real content
of that mystery, whether, in short, the proper *locus* of
Mariology is not primarily, if not exclusively, in liturgy and
prayer? To many Orthodox it seems that a theological "cu-
riosity" concerning Mary may in fact constitute one of the
sources of a certain onesidedness of Western Mariology...
But before we reach any conclusions, however tentative, we
shall first give a brief description of the place of Mary in the
Orthodox liturgical tradition, then say a few words about
the development of the veneration of the Mother of God,
and finally, try to formulate a more or less synthetic view
of its theological significance.

I

There are four main expressions of Mariology in the
Byzantine liturgy:

(a) *The Mariological prayers*—As a general rule each
cycle of liturgical prayers has always at its conclusion a
special prayer addressed to Mary. Thus, for example, the
groups of hymns (*stichera*) which we find within the
fixed structure of the daily services are always closed
with the so-called *theotokion*, which follows the doxol-
ogy "Glory to the Father, the Son and the Holy Spirit,
now and ever and unto ages of ages." This rule applies to
all liturgical units: the daily, weekly, and yearly cycles,
as well as the Sanctoral. Whatever the theme of any
particular celebration, its last word, its seal will always
be the Theotokos, Mary—the Virgin Mother of God.

(b) *Mariological feasts*—There exists within the liturgy a highly developed cycle of Mariological commemorations. Four of them: the Nativity of the Virgin (September 8), the Presentation of the Theotokos in the Temple (November 21), Annunciation (March 25), and Dormition (August 15) belong to the category of the twelve major feasts. The feast of the Presentation of Christ in the Temple (February 2)—of the same category—is also deeply Mariological. In addition to these major feasts, we find a number of lesser Mariological feasts such as: the Protection of the Virgin (October 1), the Synaxis of the Theotokos (December 26), and the Conception of Mary (December 9), etc.

(c) *Mariological iconography*—The icons of the Theotokos are an integral part of an Orthodox Church, where their very position—in the apse and on the iconostasis—has definite theological meaning. One must add to this a tremendously developed cult of the so-called "miraculous icons" of the Theotokos. Russia alone had more than 300 of such "revealed" icons—each of which also has its day of celebration and a liturgical "proper." Some of these icons' feasts—as for example that of the icon of *Our Lady of Kazan* in Russia, or *Zoodohos Peghe* (Life-Giving Fountain) in Greece, have developed into major and extremely popular feasts.

d) *Para-liturgical Mariology piety*—Together with this "official" Mariological material in liturgy one must mention the enormous amount of secondary or para-liturgical Mariological feasts and services. The collection of the various "*akathistoi*" to Mary—written after the pattern of the famous Byzantine *Akathistos*—would fill several volumes and is very typical of the constantly renewed flow of warm piety, love and praise addressed to Mary.

Not all of these materials are, to be sure, of equal value and quality. Yet, the best Byzantine hymnographers—St John of Damascus, St Andrew of Crete, St Cosmas of Maioum, etc.—wrote some of their greatest compositions on Mariological themes, and it is in their works that one finds the true expression, the true contemplation and understanding of Mary in the Orthodox tradition.

Finally and not less important is the elaboration of these themes in the homilies composed for Mariological feasts by the Byzantine Fathers and doctors.

II

There exists no comprehensive history of the veneration of Mary in the Eastern Church and, therefore, only a few and "preliminary" remarks can be made. It seems that the first liturgical expression of that veneration must have been the so-called "concomitant" feasts, i.e., celebrations attached to the major feasts of Christ. The first Mariological feast may have been the *Synaxis* of December 26—directly connected with the celebration of Christ's Nativity. Annunciation was at first the name given to the Sunday before Christmas, etc. All this points to the basically Christological dimension of the veneration of Mary, the contemplation by the Church of her place within the mystery of Incarnation. Even today the main Byzantine icon of Mary is that of the Mother with the Child—which is for the Orthodox Church primarily an icon of Incarnation.

The second remark concerns the biblical expression of Mariological themes. Of special interest here is the application to Mary of the entire terminology of the Temple and its cultic symbolism. The Temple and all its sacred furnishings are always understood by Byzantine hymnographers and preachers as announcing and foretelling the various "dimensions" of the mystery of Mary. She is the Temple, the Door, the Candlestick, the Censer, the Holy of Holies, etc. In this context even the "non-biblical" feasts—such as the Nativity of the Virgin or the Presentation in the Temple, are fundamentally the "fruit" of a certain reading and understanding of the Old Testament.

In the third place, one must stress the origin of certain Mariological feasts as rooted in the construction and dedication of churches in various places in which events of the sacred history were supposed to have taken place.

Thus, when investigating the history of Mariological piety, one discovers that it is rooted not in any special revelation but, primarily, in the experience of liturgical worship. In other terms, it is not a theological reflection on Mary that gave birth to her veneration; it is the liturgy as the experience of "heaven on earth," as communion with and the knowledge of heavenly realities, as an act of love and adoration, that little by little revealed the unique place of Christ's Mother in both the economy of salvation and the mystery of the "world to come." Mary is not part of the Church's *kerygma*, whose only content is Christ. She is the inner secret of the Church as communion with Christ. The Church preaches Christ, not Mary. But communion with Christ reveals Mary as the secret joy within the Church. "In her," says a hymn, "rejoices all creation."

This "cultic" or liturgical origin of Mariology is of special importance for the understanding of its true nature and theological implications. For, in a sense, Mary is not the object of a particular cult, added, so to speak, to that of Christ. She is, rather, an essential "dimension" of the cult addressed to God and Christ, a quality or tonality of that cult. To understand this, one must briefly enumerate the more important Mariological themes of the Byzantine liturgy.

III

If Christ is the new Adam, Mary is very often referred to as the *new Eve*. This reveals the first—soteriological—dimension of her veneration by the Church. The Church has concentrated in Mary the whole biblical vision and experience of the relationship between God and creation, the Savior and the world, as a mystery of love whose closest expression in "this world" is the man-woman relationship. God loves the world, God loves the chosen people, Christ loves the Church as the husband loves his wife; or, to be more exact, the mystery of human love reflects the mystery of God's love for His creation. Mary stands thus for the *femininity* of creation itself, femininity meaning here: responding love, obedience, self-giving, the readiness to live exclusively in, and for, the Other... Eve failed for she took the initiative, she distorted thus the ontological order of creation and became the cause of sin. The chosen people of God failed to be the "handmaid" of the Lord in love and obedience. It is, therefore, Mary who, by her total obedience, restores something absolutely essential in the order of creation. The light of an eternal spring comes to us when on the day of the Annunciation we hear the decisive: "Behold, I am the handmaid of the Lord; let it be to me according to your word! (Lk 1:38). This is indeed the whole creation, the whole mankind and each one of us, acknowledging the works which express our ultimate nature and being, our acceptance to be the *bride of God*, our betrothal to the One who from all eternity loved us." Mary is not the representative of the woman or women before God, she is the icon of the entire creation, the whole mankind as response to Christ and to God. This is well expressed in the traditional icon of Mary—"*platitera ton ouranon*" "more spacious than heaven") which is so often found in the apse of Byzantine churches.

IV

Being the heart of the new creation, Mary is the icon of Christ. The Church is institution and the Church is life. Ecclesiology, as it developed since the Reformation and the Counter-Reformation, dealt almost exclusively with the *institutional* aspect of the Church, which is its "masculine" aspect: canonical and jurisdictional structures, hierarchy, *ordos*, etc. All this is necessary and essential for the Church; all this, however, is not *the* Church! The Church is new life in Christ, new joy, communion, love, ascension, deification, peace. The Church is an eternal "passage"— from the old into the new, from this world into the Kingdom of God. It is difficult to define this life, but those who live it, be it only imperfectly, know that its perfect expression, its very "movement," is Mary. As life, the Church is a *she*, the Bride of Christ, the one who is called from eternity to be "a chaste virgin to Christ" (2 Cor 11:2), to whom from all eternity her Bridegroom has said: "thou art all fair, my love, there is no spot in thee." No synod, no ecclesiastical authority, has decreed all this; it is the direct and living experience of the Church herself that has discovered this identification of the Church with Mary, has expressed the life of the Church in reference to Mary and the veneration of Mary in reference to the Church. The piety of the Church is Mariological because Mary is the very embodiment of that piety, its image, its direction, its movement. She is the "oranta"—the one eternally alive in adoration and self-giving....

V

The icon of creation, the icon of the Church, Mary is also "the dawn of the mysterious day"—the foretaste of the Kingdom of God, the presence amoung us of that "realized eschatology" which is so often mentioned by theologians. From what secret source did the Church learn that the one who is "virgin after childbearing" is also "alive after death"? (Kontakion of the Feast of the Dormition). Yet it is a certitude, a self-evidence of the faith that, even before the common resurrection and the consummation of all things in Christ, She is fully alive, i.e., beyond the destruction and the separation of death.

The Christian East has never rationalized this mystery, has not expressed it within the categories of original sin, immaculate conception, *donum superadditum*, etc. Different in this from Western Mariology, it affirms that Mary shared original sin with mankind and that she fell asleep—i.e., died... The wonderful thing about her is not that, having no original sin, she did not have to die, but that her death itself was filled to capacity with life in God, and, therefore, changed into "blessed assumption." It is her total unity with Christ that destroyed her death and made her the beginning, the inauguration of the common resurrection. In her, a part of this world is totally glorified and deified, and she is thus the "dawn of the mysterious day" of the Kingdom.

VI

She stood at the Cross. A sword pierced through her soul "that thoughts out of many hearts may be revealed" (Lk 2:35). She was made our Mother by her crucified Son. Every Wednesday and Friday the Church remembers Mary's mystery of suffering and compassion and expresses it in its beautiful *stavrotheotokia* (the Byzantine counterparts of the *Stabat Mater Dolorosa*...). This is the source of another dimension of Mariology—the expression of Mary as protection and intercession. She is identified with all suffering, with human life in this world as tragedy and suffering. She is thus the icon of the Church as Mother. This theme is nowhere better expressed than in the feast of the Protection of the Virgin and in the unquenchable flow of Mariological prayers mentioned above in the category of para-liturgical services and compositions.

Summing up, we can say once more that the "cult" of Mary is not an autonomous element in the rich tradition of the Church, an element that can be studied "in itself." It is an essential dimension of Christian cosmology, anthropology, ecclesiology and eschatology. It is not an object of faith, but its fruit; not a *nota ecclesiae*, but the self-revelation of the Church; not even a doctrine, but the life and fragrance of Christian doctrine in us.